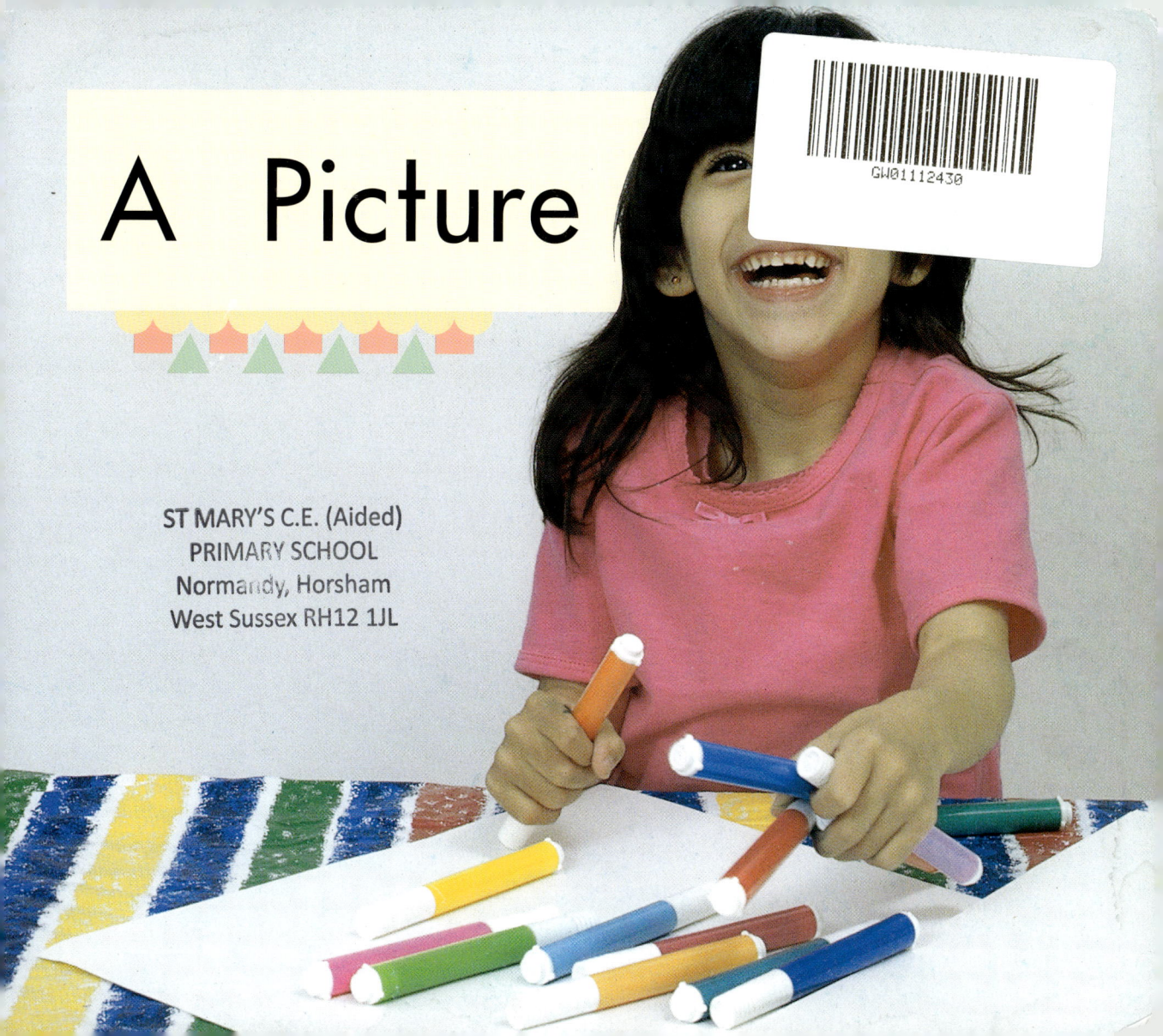

I can make a circle.

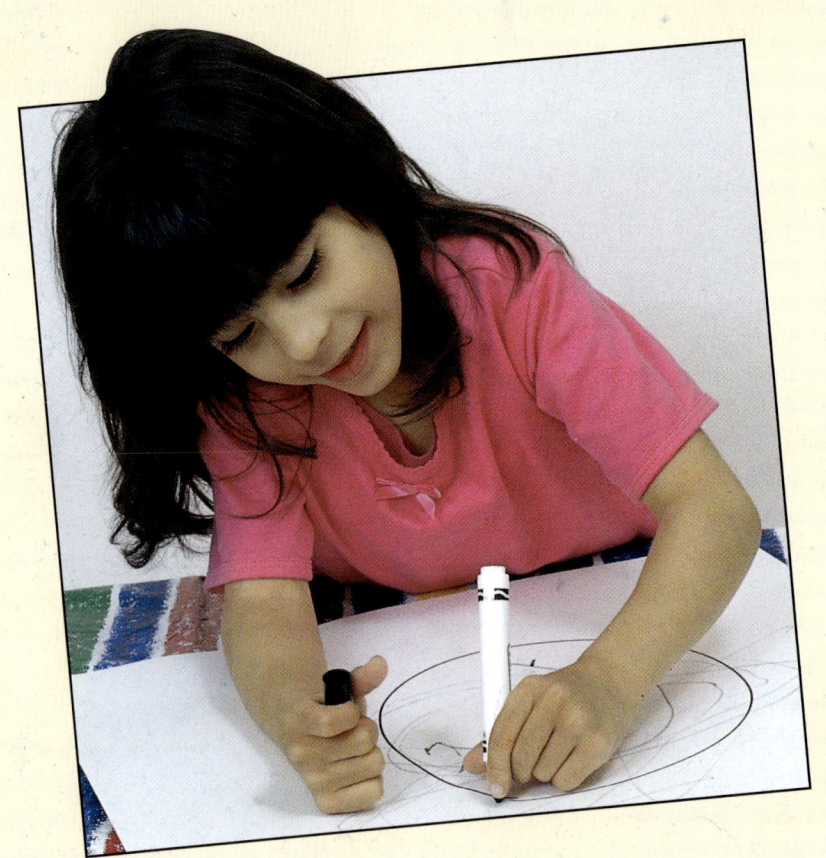

3

So I can make a balloon.

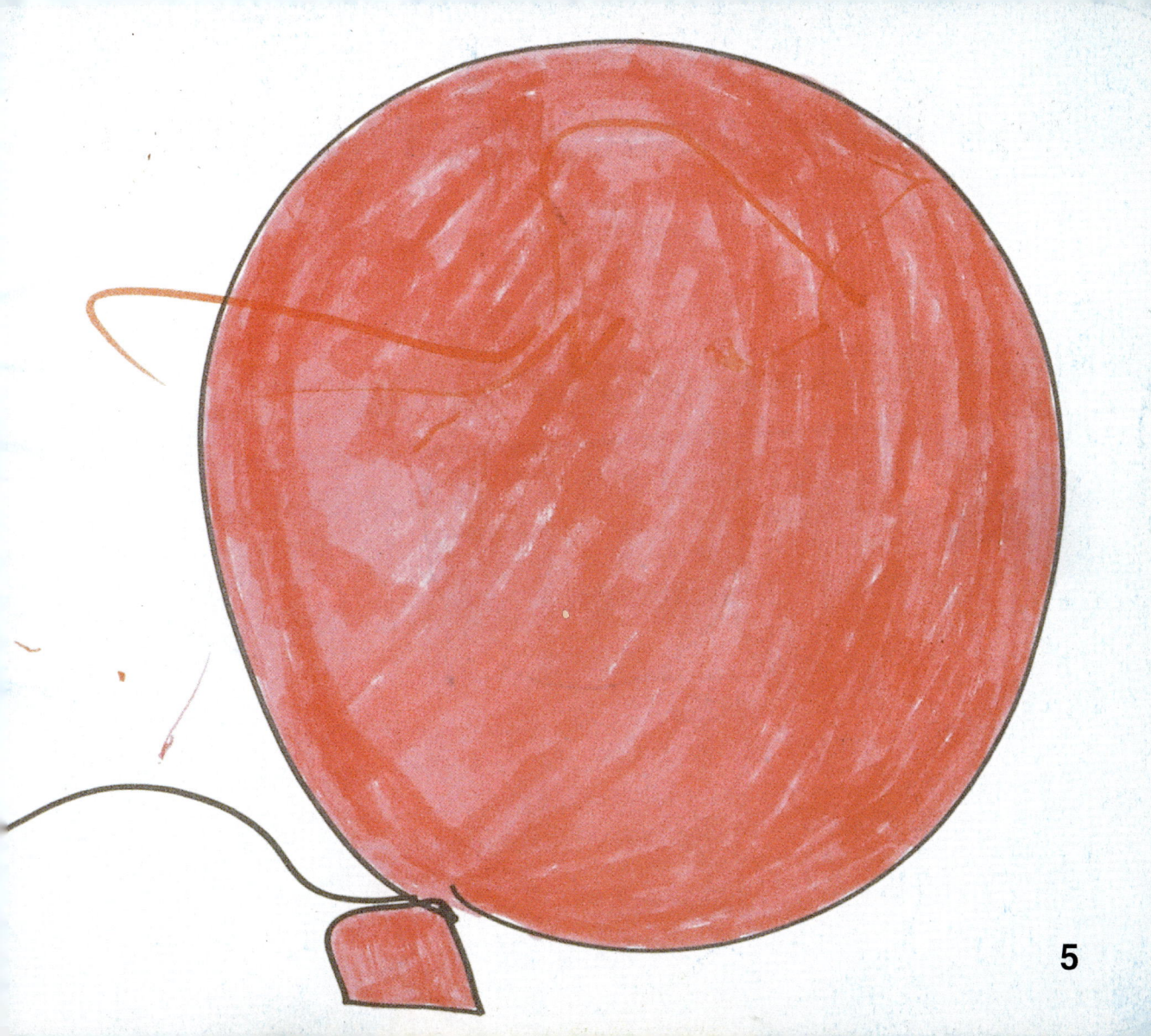

I can make a triangle.

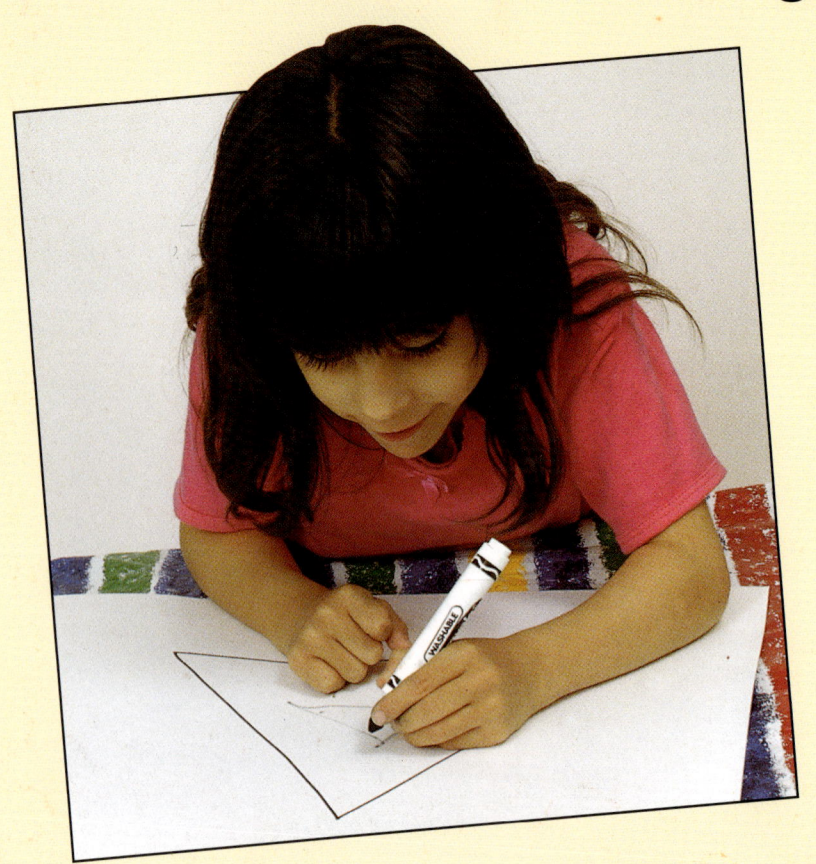

So I can m

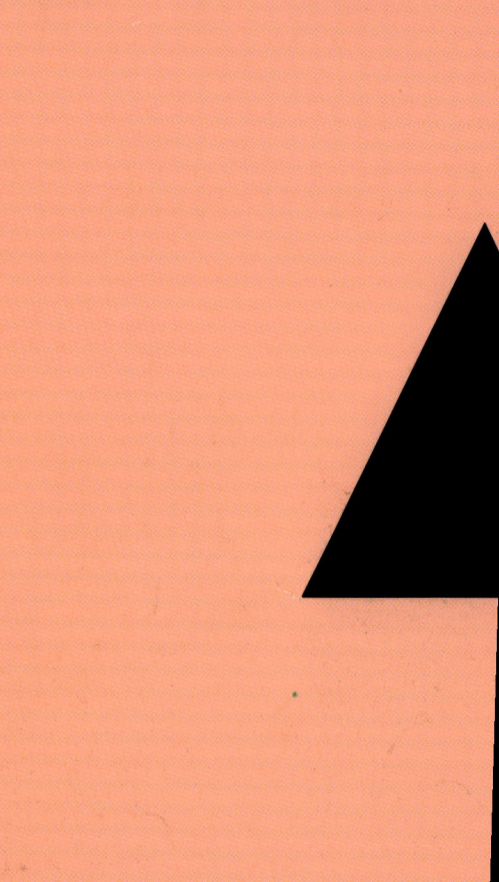

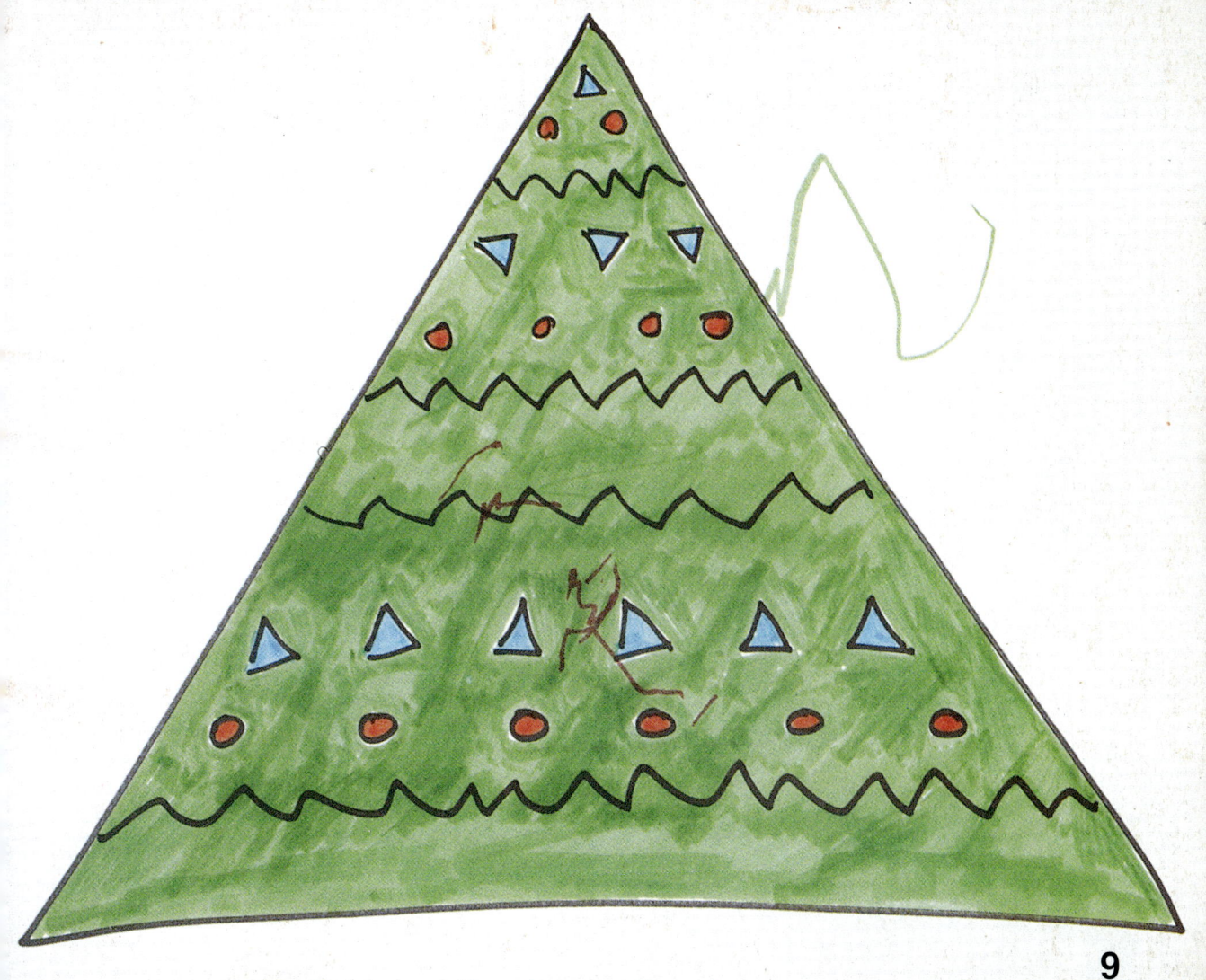

I can make a square.

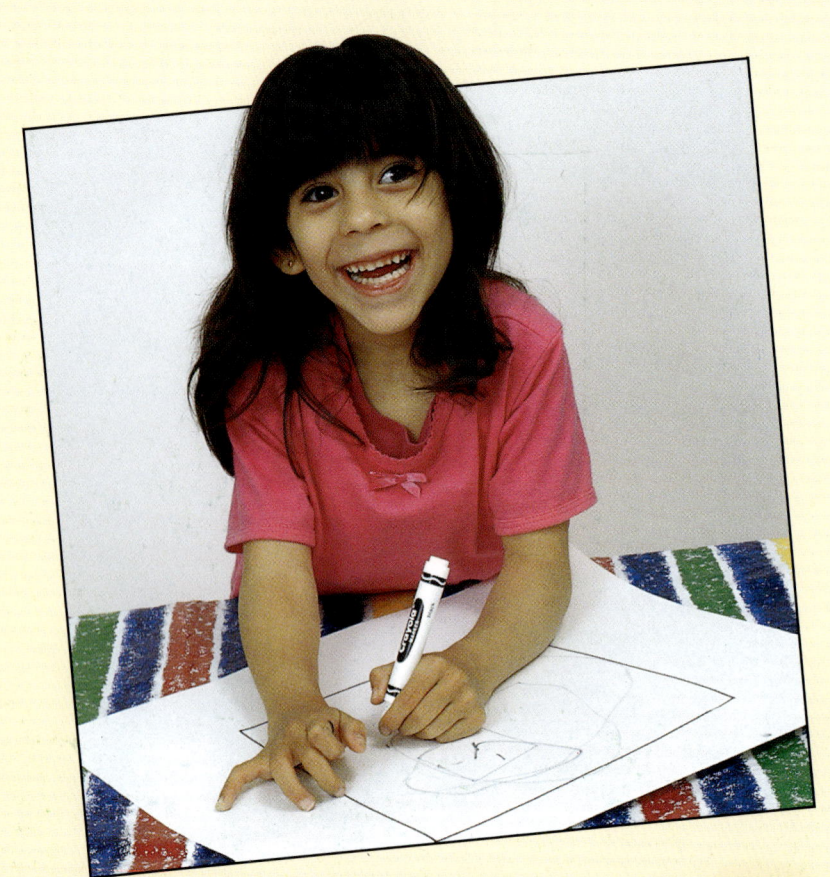

So I can make a present.

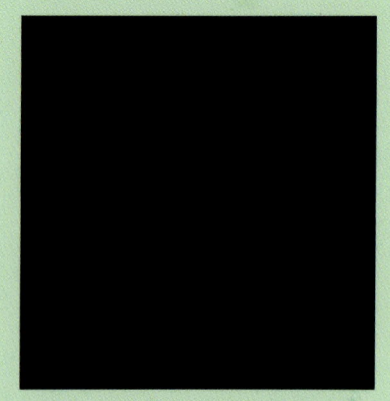

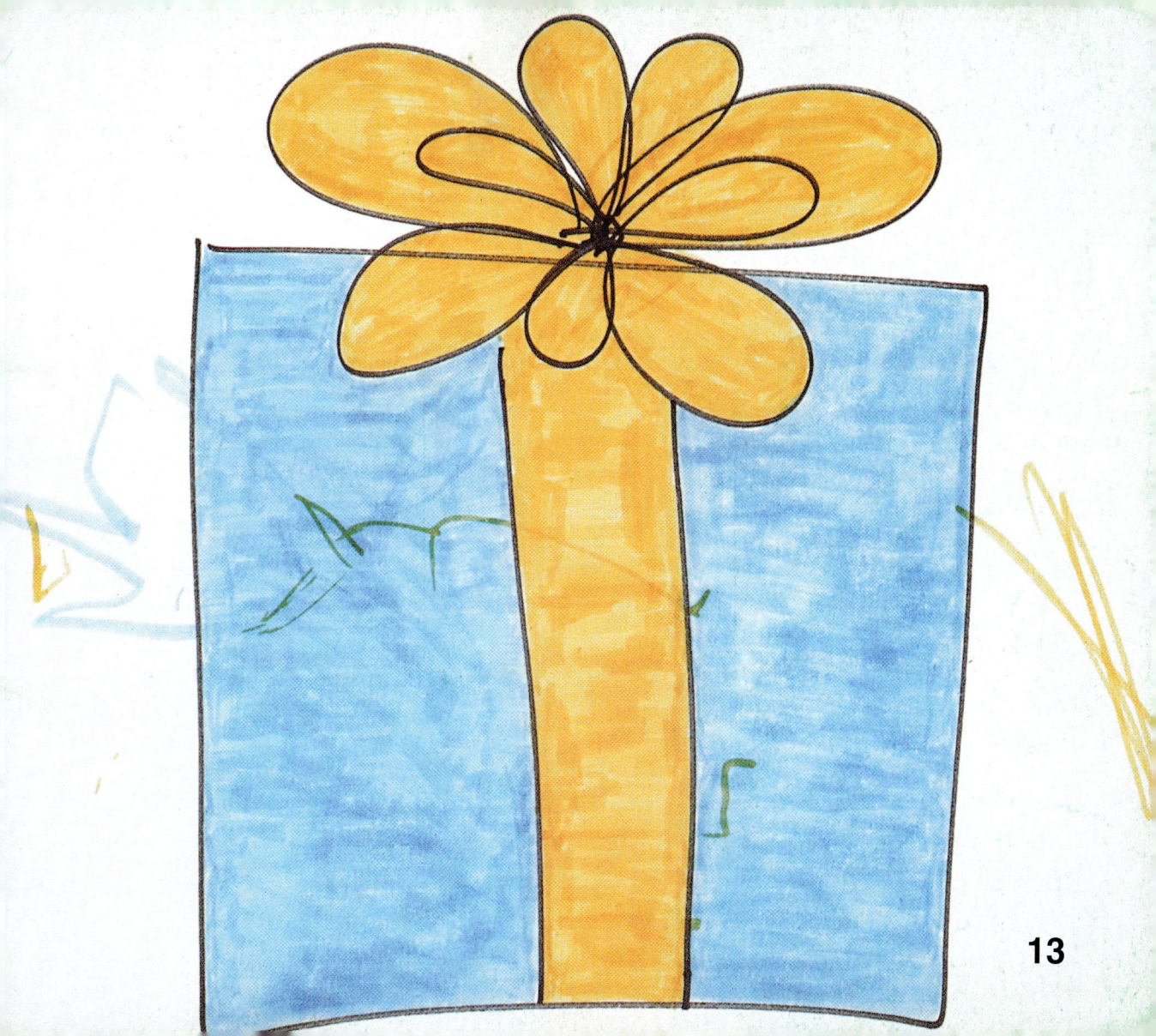

I can make a circle,
a triangle, and a square.
So I can make a picture.

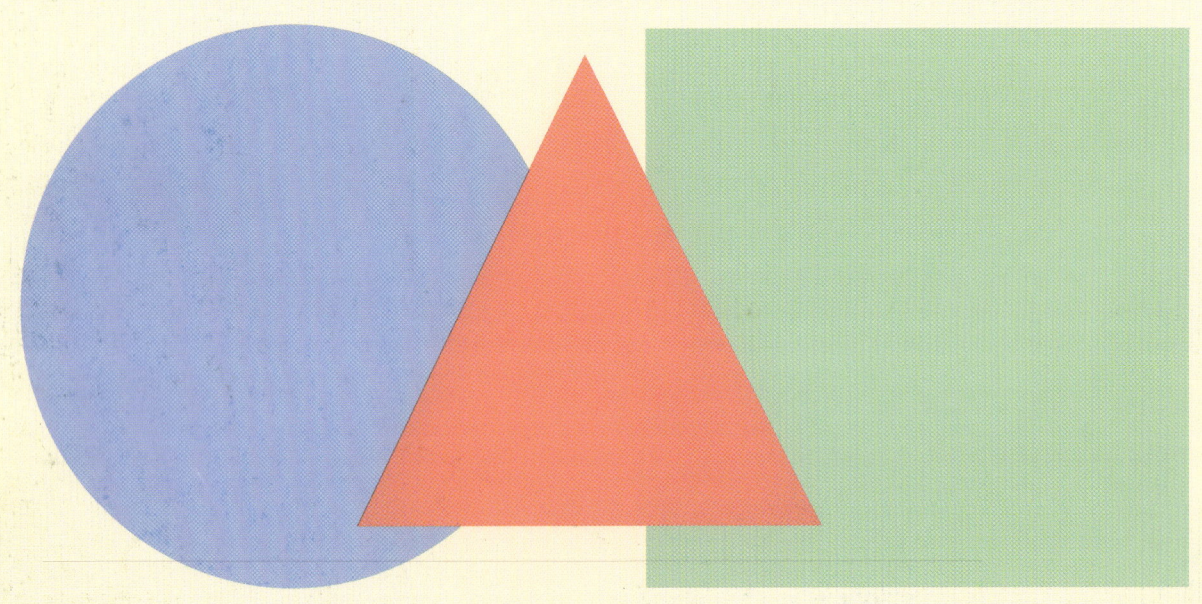

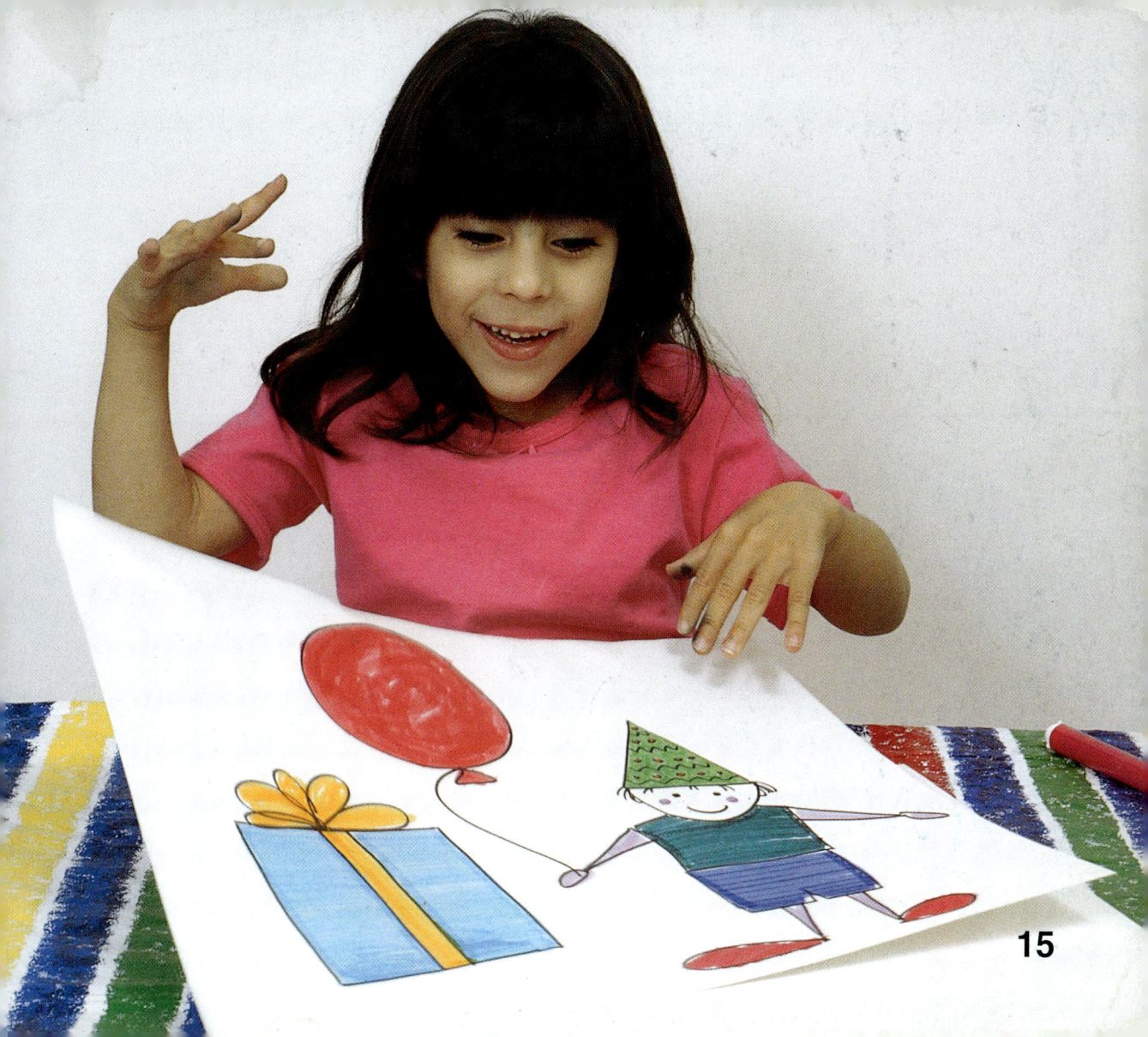

Here are some other things I can make.

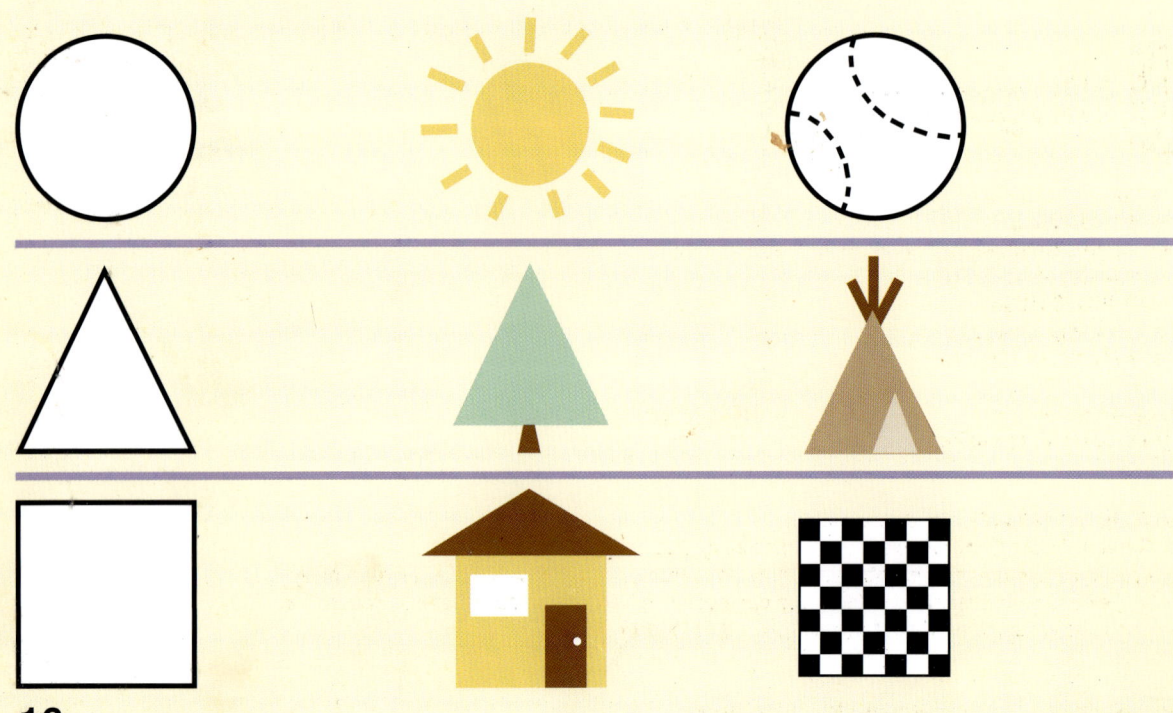